THE DISCIPLINE

OF

KINGDOM

ADVANCEMENT

How to Move from
Kingdom Talk
to
Kingdom Walk

THE DISCIPLINE

OF

KINGDOM

ADVANCEMENT

How to Move from
Kingdom Talk
to
Kingdom Walk

Michelle Walker-Wade

The Discipline of Kingdom Advancement
How to Move from Kingdom Talk to Kingdom Walk
by Michelle Walker-Wade
© 2017, Michelle Walker-Wade
admin@mwalkerwade.com

Published by Anointed Fire™ House
www.anointedfirehouse.com
Cover Design by Anointed Fire™ House

ISBN-10: 0-9982507-8-3

ISBN-13: 978-0-9982507-8-6

I have tried to recreate events, locales and conversations from my memories of them. In order to maintain their anonymity in some instances I have changed the names of individuals and places, I may have changed some identifying characteristics and details such as physical properties, occupations and places of residence.

Although the author and publisher have made every effort to ensure that the information in this book was correct at press time, the author and publisher do not assume and hereby disclaim any liability to any party for any loss, damage, or disruption caused by errors or omissions, whether such errors or omissions result from negligence, accident, or any other cause.

Table of Contents

Dedication

I dedicate this book to my God and King for His continued faithfulness.

To my loving husband, Pastor Alonzo Wade, and to the best mother in the world, Mom Mary. You are my best supporters and constant encouragers. Thank you for enduring all of my *quirks*.

To my brothers, nieces, nephews, and my bigger than life family: The Colemans and the Colters. You are a nation of leaders and lovers of God. You make failure *not an option*.

Finally, to the men and women of God who invested time and prayers into my spiritual maturity and development as a leader down through the years.

Those who poured into me from my youth: Bishop Earnestine Cleveland-Reems, Apostles John Chandler and China Cleveland, Apostle Christine Liddell, and my beloved who is now resting in God, Chaplain "Aunt" Mary Lance.

And to those who helped me through some very tough times to continue growing personally and in the ministry of our Lord, Apostle Cynthia L. Chess, Dr. Anthony G. Majors and Dr. Avis E. Hinkson. I love you all. My life is blessed because of the Holy Spirit working in you.

Chapter 1

The Challenger's Voice Cries Out

There's something interesting about *a voice crying out in the wilderness*. It's loud. It's radical, and by implication, it must be willing and able to stand on its own. It goes against the grain and infuriates the norm, and then, it paves the path for a better way.

It was somewhere around June 1985 when a group of five extraordinarily skilled engineers cried out: "Please don't do it." The most memorable amongst this team of professionals was Roger Boisjoly. His voice cried out the longest and the loudest, and his convictions, coupled with substantiating data to back up his theory, were the strongest. The *Space Shuttle Challenger STS-51-L*, with its rocket boosters inadequately designed to work properly in cold weather, was a catastrophe waiting to happen. "The problem,

Boisjoly wrote, was the elastic seals at the joints of the multi-stage booster rockets. They tended to stiffen and unseal in cold weather and NASA's ambitious shuttle launch schedule included winter lift-offs with risky temperatures, even in Florida."[1]

Boisjoly worked as a top mechanical, aerodynamicist engineer for Morton Thiokol, the manufacturer of the solid rocket boosters for the Space Shuttle program. Because of his extensive experience, research, and data collection on the mechanics of the rocket booster, he was certain that his catastrophic prediction about the ill-fated *Challenger* was correct. In the six months leading up to a winter launch, Boisjoly repeatedly spoke up, "trying to get his concerns to be taken seriously."[2] He eventually became the voice no one wanted to hear. NASA wanted so badly to launch on time, because Congress and the general public had grown tired of waiting for them to make good on their promises to start a bus service to space, that they eventually strong-armed

Morton Thiokol's management to agree to launch the Challenger despite their own engineers' expert advice.[3]

The arguments continued right up until the night before the launch on January 28, 1986. Roger Boisjoly, in total despondence, told his wife, "We're going to launch tomorrow and kill the astronauts."[4] The next morning, even though icicles 18 inches long had formed on the shuttle, NASA went along with their launch plan, only delaying it for a few hours in order to allow the ice to melt.

With a crowd of on-lookers cheering, the *Space Shuttle Challenger* successfully launched towards space, but it only took 73 seconds for those cheers to turn into shock, tears, and a cacophony of mourning cries. Boisjoly's worst fear became a reality. The *Challenger* exploded and all seven astronauts on-board, including the first school teacher to head into space, Christa McAuliffe, were gone forever.

When the time came for Roger Boisjoly's testimony at the commission's hearing, Morton Thiokol's lawyers gave him strict instructions on how to respond to the questions he would be asked, but Boisjoly, full of anguish and righteous conviction, went against those instructions and told the whole truth. He became what the callous systems of this world call: "a whistle-blower." [4]

Ousted from his professional network, Boisjoly resiliently took on a new mission, traveling around the world and communicating through correspondence, educating up-and-coming engineers on ethical decision-making. He kept up as much as possible with the goings-on at NASA, and years later when the Columbia Space Shuttle was to suffer a similar fate for some of the same reasons, NASA engineers secretly contacted him for ethical advice. Roger Boisjoly, referred to as a religious man who loved his family, church and country[5,7] continued this work right up until he died of cancer at age 73 on January 6, 2012.[6]

Roger Boisjoly is a perfect example of a voice crying out in the wilderness. He was disciplined, a top craftsman in his field, and a humble lover of God who used his gifts and influence to bring the uprightness of God's character into a dark place. Had he not stood as the voice, the world may have never known the truth, and furthermore, thousands of engineering practitioners and students would be void of Kingdom influence in their industry. Boisjoly was there to coach them through some of the tough moral dilemmas relevant to their discipline. Boisjoly is now gone, but what he stood for lives on in the hearts and minds of many.

Whenever I coach an individual through a life situation, I sincerely hope that person will grow to a place where they're so disciplined that eventually they will rarely need my help. This is a person who has matured in the art and skill of *wisdom in the moment.* It's much easier to talk about what to do or what could have been done when you're not in the moment, but ultimately, what counts is what you actually DO when that challenging moment presents itself. All of our teaching, training and practicing will be validated or negated right in that moment. Will you control your thoughts, your actions, and your words right there in the moment? If you're going to achieve any goal or work any plan that's set before you, you'll have to become very comfortable with constant and consistent discipline. You will grow strong in your ability to ignore distractions and other competing desires by focusing fully on your desired outcome – your predetermined goal. Remember success does not happen in a straight line. It's a zig-zag and it takes discipline to stay with it!

Chapter 2

Discipline: The Act of Training Your Soulish Man

Generally, discipline is a three step process. First, you're taught which decisions and choices will lead to a particular outcome. Next, you're trained and retrained how to make the decisions and choices that will result in the attainment of the desired outcome. After that, you'll acquire an innate tendency to make the right choice at any given moment in time. Of these three steps, only one of them can be taught to you by someone else and that's step number one. A teacher, ministry leader, or mentor can do their best to explain and discuss situations with you, hoping you'll accept the lesson and apply it to your life, but it's not until the opportunity presents itself that you'll be able to put the teaching to practice. This is training. This is when we find out if you can handle the pressure of making the right decision. What will you do if it does not work out as expected? This time in training (self-training) is critical to your development. Discipline is self-developed; no one can go through the training period for you. By definition, discipline is: "training that develops self-control or character." As you experience and acknowledge the joys of right choices, you develop wisdom for living in a way that protects you from the consequences of wrong choices. This satisfaction leads you right to step three of the process and that is: the acquisition of an innate tendency to make right choices at any moment in time. I called this *wisdom in the moment.*

Discipline is the act of training your soulish man – that is your mind, will, and emotions - how to habitually respond to internal desires and external influences. As a follower of Christ, you should make it a point to study your own patterns of behavior. Think about how you respond to feelings of pain, jealousy, fear, or disrespect. How do you respond to your spouse, pastoral leaders, and even co-workers when you don't like the way they've treated you? Do you consider your own actions first, or are you quick to criticize another person's actions? How do you behave when your money is in short supply? How do you behave on payday? How do you respond to unexpected changes?

When training your soulish man to remain focused and to use wisdom in the moment, there are two questions you should ask yourself:

1) What emotions am I feeling? How am I responding to those emotions or feelings?
2) How well will my response help me to achieve my predetermined goal?

Jesus chose 12 disciples whom He charged with the goal of initiating the grassroots movement that would reconcile the world back to God. From the time they were called until their death, and even still today, Jesus Christ and His original 12 set the patterns of behaviors for us as descendant believers to follow. The scriptures do not show us perfect men; they show us real men. We see their humanness as well as their Godlikeness.

Consider Simon Peter, who was so swift and impulsive that he did not stop and think before attempting to rebuke Jesus when He spoke of His sufferings. In response, Jesus, the master teacher, rebuked Peter, speaking to him in the sternest words He'd ever used when speaking to His disciples (Matthew 16:21-23; Mark 8:31-33). Again, it was Simon Peter who, under a sudden impulse, completely cut off the ear of Malchus. He did this right in the presence of the betrayer, Judas Iscariot, Caiaphas, the chief priest, and an army of 300 plus armed soldiers who had come to take Jesus away. Malchus was Caiaphas's public relations officer. The words he spoke publicly on behalf of Caiaphas infuriated Simon Peter so much so that he behaved impulsively and violently towards him. Simon Peter, a man who walked closer to Jesus Christ in the flesh than any other person ever will, displayed unbridled, undisciplined anger (John 18, Luke 22).

While you and I, as 21st century believers, may not go so far as to sever a body part from someone whose actions move us to anger, we may act out in less obvious, less aggressive ways. Maybe we're conveniently passive-aggressive. Think about the emotions you feel. Think about your response: your attitude, your knee-jerk opinion, or your actions. How well do you match-up to Jesus' response to this same scenario? Jesus knew His time and purpose; He focused on His predetermined plan. In that moment, he rebuked Simon Peter once again, healed Caiaphas's injury, and went on as a captive of those who'd come to take Him away.

Simon Peter wasn't all bad. In fact, he was actually so dedicated to his Kingdom advancement calling that he learned and grew very strong in grace. He had a revelation of Christ's deity that was so sharp that the Church – the

Body of Christ – was built on his confession. As an apostle, Peter taught temperance, patience, kindness and love. You see, your behavioral flaws do not disqualify you from your Kingdom calling. God knows your strengths and He knows exactly which group or community of people you can bring the influence of His Kingdom to through your servitude. God puts you in places where you can be taught which decisions and choices will help you get there, and in positions where you can practice and train how to make wise choices right in the moment. All the while, God is working on renewing your mind – working patterns of discipline in you - so He can elevate you and activate you in your predestined sphere of influence. You simply need to know that there is, in fact, a specific Kingdom call for your life and you need to be yielded to the process, come what may.

Chapter 3

Precisely What Is "Kingdom Advancement?"

My husband and I have spent many days and long car rides discussing the concept of "Kingdom advancement." We needed a concise, yet comprehensive definition that we could use as a foundation for the many teachings to come on this subject. The definition needed to be easily understood, easy to memorize, and easy to visualize.

For years, the Church has proclaimed the idea of "Kingdom advancement," but we've struggled to produce anything much different than church as usual with a flair of entertainment. From the evidence I see in our society, we may be more engaged in "Kingdom retrogression" than advancement. Since the early 2000s, the first day of the week has been noted as *Sunday Funday*[1] ... the only holiday that occurs more than once a year. It's a day you can easily find the best brunch buffets with unlimited Champagne and Mimosas. It's a big day for sport events, beach parties, park festivities and family gatherings. Unless you were raised with the habit of going to church on Sunday mornings, it's hard to make the mental shift from Sunday Funday to Sunday morning worship service. I'm not suggesting that we stop emphasizing attendance at the weekly worship service, but we do need to recognize the role that Sunday mornings play (and does not play) in the bigger picture of Kingdom advancement.

According to our definition, *Kingdom advancement* is: intentionally taking the character of God, which you noticeably carry once you've been redeemed and transformed by Christ, to those who do not live by it, and doing so in such a way that your influence gradually shifts their lifestyle practices and behaviors.

Kingdom advancement is not straight-line evangelism; neither is it outreach. We tend to use the terms evangelism and outreach synonymously, but they're actually two different functions.

Evangelism is "the act of spreading the gospel, preaching the gospel, and teaching men how to avail themselves to the offer of salvation."[2]

The word "evangelism" comes from the same Greek words as "gospel" and "good news." Where there is good news, there's usually bad news as well. The ministry of evangelism must create a picture of both. The bad news is: sin is an offense against God and for it, you will be judged. The good news is: if you confess your sins and repent (turn and go in a different direction), you'll be completely washed clean from previous sins and won't be judged because of them. The good and the bad news are both part of the gospel message that must be preached. Evangelism is loving, but it's confrontational too.

Outreach, on the other hand, is "reaching out to the community in order to meet needs".[3] It is an act of love that allows non-believers to make a connection with the Church and experience the love of Christ. While outreach involves reaching out to communities, regions, and nations, it doesn't necessarily require preaching the good news.

Outreach makes the Church visibly known for being a resource to help meet the practical and physical needs of people. Outreach alone will not result in the saving of souls, however, it often leads to an evangelism opportunity and this may result in repentance and acceptance of Christ. In doing the work of outreach, we should let people know the reason for our actions is to simply share the love of Christ.

I have often observed well-intended Christians spreading the gospel in the most condemnatory of ways. While evangelism must include some degree of expression of God's dissatisfaction with our sinful behavior, we should gradually release words of correction in this way:

1. During outreach – No words of correction.
2. During evangelism – Few words of correction; just enough for the person to acknowledge their sins and to desire to repent from them.
3. During discipleship – gradually released words of instruction that help the new convert develop and mature spiritually.

In Matthew 28:19-20, Jesus said: "Go make disciples of all nations" - NATIONS, not just people, but *people-groups* such as those who live together, or work together, play together or who collaborate together. You see, salvation is an individual action of one single person, but discipleship is most effective when it happens in a group of people because the goal of true discipleship is transformation. Transformation is most effective and enduring when it happens in small communities of people because there's strength in numbers.

The King James Version of Matthew 28:19-20 states this:

"Go ye therefore, and **teach** *(mathēteuō) all nations, baptizing them in the name of the Father, and of the Son, and of the Holy Ghost:* **Teaching** *(didaskō) them to observe all things whatsoever I have commanded you..."*

"Teach" in verse 19, comes from the Greek word *mathēteuō (G3100)*, which means: to be a *disciple* of one; to follow his precepts, guidelines and instructions. *Mathēteuō* is the teaching that aims to develop Christ-like lifestyles, beliefs and practices. We know someone is a disciple of another person because they begin to act and behave like that person. Jesus Christ had (and has) disciples; Galileo had disciples. ISIS is a group of disciples. Hinduism, Buddhism, Satanism and so on all have disciples.[4] Jesus commanded us to teach, progressively over time, all people and all nations to live morally and behave like Him, not to strip away their cultural expressions, but to develop and display His character in daily life. There should be an obvious distinction between you and me as disciples of Christ versus those who are not His disciples. *Mathēteuō* is the teaching that grows us up in lifestyle choices.

On the other hand, "teach," in verse 20, comes from the Greek word *didaskō (G1321),* which means to teach the scriptures (or the Word of God) by holding *didactic discourses* in order to instruct and instill scriptural doctrine, laws, and commandments. *Didaskō* denotes a teaching style that involves interaction, dialog, and even debate. *Didactic,* more or less, pertains to the teaching of scriptural laws and commandments (as opposed to Bible-based historical stories) in order to convey moral truths. In this scripture, Jesus' instructions are for us to teach new believers to *do* (or live in accordance with) the commandments and laws that He's already taught us to do.

These teachings, the *mathēteuō* and the *didaskō,* are the bedrocks of character transformation and the foundations of Kingdom advancement. Those who are willing to sacrifice the time required to receive and become engaged with this type of revolutionary teaching are the only ones who will have a divine revelation of the Kingdom of Heaven and a strong enough conviction to advance it. Jesus Christ made a clear point in the 13th chapter of Matthew that many will hear, but few will adhere to. And only those who adhere will advance. Kingdom advancement is all about intentionally transforming others through the impact of your influence.

Chapter 4

Transformation Happens When We Teach What Jesus Said to Teach

The fact that God actually has expectations of His children seems to elude us at times. We want to take in all of God's love, mercy and grace, yet we deny living out the disciplines of His expectations. Jesus said, "Teach them to do all I have commanded of you." Commandments are laws and rules that govern our conduct and choices. When you fail to observe (or obey) Jesus' commandments, you make wrong choices; but when you follow them, God rewards your faithfulness. God knows sometimes it is hard to obey Him. He knows the enemy dispatches situations and challenges to test your commitment. The enemy's goal is and always will be to get you to fail, to miss the mark, and to sin. This is why discipleship is a process that occurs with many teachings over time. If we evangelize unbelievers to repentance, but then fail to teach them by *didactic discourse* and do not ensure they've received the baptism of the Holy Spirit, our jobs are not yet complete. The new convert has not been taught and trained to observe Jesus' commandments; the commandments which He received from God, the Father. Sadly, many long-term church attending believers do not observe to do all Jesus commanded either. The thrust of real **Kingdom advancement** can only happen when believers excel **in living out the commandments and principals Jesus spoke of**. These Kingdom principals are an important part of what Jesus taught and preached when He was in the Earth (Matthew 4:23, Matthew 9:35, Mark 1:14-15, Luke 4:43).

I'm not going to elaborate on these laws, but I will list 35 of them below. As a follower of Christ, you should study and meditate on these commandments, and pray them through until your mind is transformed and your lifestyle shows the evidence of that transformation. Then you can teach others to do likewise.

35 Things Jesus Commanded His Followers To Do

1. Be the light so those who are in darkness can understand that your goodness is because of your relationship with God (Matthew 5:14-16).
2. Be first to go and resolve every issue with your brother or sister; don't wait for them to come to you (Matthew 5: 21-26).
3. Get rid of anything that causes you to sin, no matter how small it may be (Matthew 5:26-30).
4. Do not make promises you cannot keep (Matthew 5:33-37).
5. Do not seek retaliation against anyone who has wronged you (Matthew 5:38-39).
6. When resolving a matter with someone, go above and beyond what is asked of you (Matthew 5: 40-42).

7. Love your enemies and pray for the people who harass you (Matthew 5:43-44).

8. Do not use God's glory or the Lord's work to draw attention to yourself (Matthew 6:1-2).

9. Pray and fast with sincerity to God, not to draw attention to yourself from man (Matthew 6:5-6, and 16).

10. Pattern your prayers after Jesus' prayer (Matthew 6:9-15).

11. Don't let the pride of life fill you with greed (Matthew 6: 19-21).

12. Desire to have the character of God and to live righteously more than you want anything else in the world (Matthew 6: 33).

13. Correct your own short-comings before you tell other people about theirs (Matthew 7:1-6, Luke 6: 39-42).

14. Do not naively believe that everyone will value what you have to offer; discern those who will thoughtlessly discard it (Matthew 7:6).

15. Treat people the same way you want them to treat you (Matthew 7:12).

16. Ask God for what you need and want. Search out His wisdom and be proactive about it (Matthew 7:7).

17. Give to the poor, take care of the needy and be hospitable to the stranger (Matthew 7:41-46).

18. Do not follow the crowd, doing what seems easy. Choose the narrow and more difficult path that leads to eternal life (Matthew 7:13-14).

19. Don't believe that everyone who says they are a prophet is a true prophet of God. Discern what's real (Matthew 7:15-20).

20. Use your God-given authority to help free others from sickness, torment and distress, and do so without taking advantage of them (Matthew 10:1, 8).

21. Do not emotionally, physically, or spiritually abuse or look down on children (Matthew 18:1-10).

22. Do not openly embarrass your brother or sister for wrongdoing. Go to them directly, and if necessary, bring in another Godly witness or take it to the leader of the church (Matthew 18:15-17).

23. Love the Lord God with all your heart, soul, and mind (Matthew 22:36).

24. Love your neighbor as yourself (Matthew 22:39).

25. Do not be arrogant. Stay humble (Matthew 23:12).

26. Go out and make disciples (Matthew 28:19-20).

27. Do not view other church or ministry groups as your competition. We're all on the same team (Mark 9:38-40).

28. Before you pray for your own needs, if you have anything against someone, forgive them (Mark 11:25-26). No matter how many times a fellow believer wrongs you, always forgive (Luke 17:3-4).

29. Be compassionate and show mercy (Luke 6:36).

30. Do not answer, "Yes Lord" unless you plan to do what He has told you to do (Luke 6:46-49).

31. Always be ready for the Lord's return (Luke 12:35-40).

32. Be reborn in the Spirit (John 3:1-8).

33. Obey God (John 14:15).

34. Stay completely intertwined in the ways and teachings of Jesus Christ (John 15:1-7).

35. Reproduce in others what Jesus Christ has produced in you (John 15:8).

When you apply these 35 teachings, it will transform your thinking and everything you do in the church, at home, at work and in the community. This is how you take Kingdom talk and create Kingdom walk. It brings the Kingdom out of the heavenly and on to the Earth where every decision you make has the power to influence how others perceive our Lord.

Chapter 5

Kingdom Advancement – A Form of Community Development?

Kingdom advancement - intentionally taking the character of God, which you noticeably carry once you've been redeemed and transformed by Christ, to those who do not live by it. You are to do so in such a way that your influence gradually shifts their lifestyle practices and behaviors. When this is done correctly, it should transform individual lives and consequently shape and develop the communities in which you live, work, and socialize. The late Dr. Myles Munroe said, "If you're going to influence society, you must be the leader in that area."[1] I would venture to say that on a large scale, the local Christian church is generally not viewed as a **leading agent** of community development. We're more so thought of as *charity **to** the com* *munity*, but not necessarily *developers* **of** the community. Charity fulfills temporary needs in the lives of people, providing short-term, quick fix responses, whereas, community development helps people and communities create and implement long-term, transformational behaviors, habits and disciplines[2]. Jesus Christ commanded His followers to be salt and light. Salt preserves and strengthens what it comes in contact with (food, for example) so that it is more enjoyable and long-lasting. Light provides the security of sight and vision (see commandment #1). Jesus Christ also told His followers to eradicate evil, confusion, and sickness in their communities (see commandment #20). Jesus commanded you to love others as well as you love yourself (see commandment #24). These are just three Kingdom advancement principals that could fuel major community development efforts. Community development is about people coming together to shape their future in such a way that it improves the quality of life for everyone in the community. It is the transforming power of God that makes you salt and light, purified and ready to show true love to others. Hebrews 10:19-24 says:

*"Therefore, brethren, since we have **confidence** to enter the holy place by the blood of Jesus, by **a new and living way** ... let us draw near with a sincere heart in full assurance of faith, having our hearts sprinkled **clean from an evil conscience and our bodies washed** with pure water. Let us hold fast the confession of our hope without wavering... and let us consider how **to stimulate one another** to love and good deeds..."*

Can you see how we should work together for everyone's good after our lives have been transformed? We're not to lord ourselves over one another, attempt to dominate or oppress one another, but rather, we should be working together to motivate one another.

Consider how Commandments #11 and #17 instruct you not to be so consumed with greed that you neglect the poor, the needy and those who need your hospitality. Greed destroys communities (Proverbs 15:27), but generosity builds them up.

Acts 2:44-47 reads:

"And all those who had believed were together and had all things in common; and ***they began selling their property and possessions and were sharing them with all, as anyone might have need***. *Day by day continuing with one mind in the temple, and breaking bread from house to house; they were taking their meals together with gladness and sincerity of heart, praising God and having favor with all the people. And the Lord was* ***adding to their number day by day*** *those who were being saved."*

These converts (or disciples) were so transformed by what they were learning from the apostles that they took responsibility for developing their own healthy communities. I believe these original apostles obediently taught all Jesus Christ had commanded them to do in Mathew 28. Yes, the apostles performed miracles, signs, and wonders as expressed in the second chapter of Acts, but what if – just what if – the more appropriate reason why the church grew day-by-day was because people saw how a community of transformed lives working together to help everyone live better, was good for all? Could it possibly be that true Kingdom advancement wanes because the five-fold apostolic church relies too heavily on miracles to draw people to God, instead of the influence of transformed lives?

I believe Christ's followers have a clear mandate to be the leading change agents in our communities, not by dominating or belittling those who don't believe, but by working alongside them, living transformed in front of them and in secret (so as not to be a pretender), and by giving them the same merciful love Christ gave us. You must be such a lover of your community that you take on the Kingdom mindset of *the* servant-leader, Jesus Christ, not coming in to make a name for yourself or to establish your own little kingdom to which everyone must fall subject. Jesus Christ came to fulfill the demands of an old unachievable law, and to provide access and opportunities for everyone to live abundantly under a new law. You can absolutely do this with the help and indwelling of your own personal counselor, the Holy Spirit.

You should live out the gospel of Christ by being in love with your community. Christ's love for mankind was so deep that He gave His whole life to serve us. He came serving and teaching leaders a new way to nurture others. He taught leaders to make leaders, telling them to teach others not to follow the crowd (commandment #18), and teach everyone to go out and make disciples (commandment #26). Christ taught them how to resolve conflict, saying, "Correct your own short-comings first" (commandment # 13) "and then go above and beyond what is asked of you in resolving a conflict with your brother" (commandment #6). The local church should be the living providers of this type of leadership development in every community its parishioners come in contact with. You should be constantly thinking of new ideas and ways to transform lives. Even as you meet various charitable needs in your community, also create opportunities to help others develop their potential, become more responsible, and rise-up as leaders of change in their own communities. I know this sounds extremely challenging, and I'd be less than honest if I told you otherwise. Jesus Christ and the original apostles were challenged by it too, thus, whenever appropriate, they would peacefully *shake the dust from their feet* and move on to the next house (Matthew10:14). You will have an opportunity to share the love of Christ in the future. Persist in prayer, meditation, and hearing the Word of God to keep you strong and determined. Give thanks to God for the Holy Spirit who comes to comfort you, give you a sound mind and empower you to do Kingdom advancement work.

Chapter 6

Personal-Development: Becoming Your God-Ordained Self for the Kingdom's Sake

Who is your *ideal-self*?[1] Who do you really want to be? What do you really believe in? What characteristics, values, goals and achievements would make up the 'perfect you'? What problem did Jehovah place you on the Earth to resolve?

Think about your *real-self* [2] for a minute. How do you think and perceive the world around you? How do you act and respond to it? Who were you brought up to be? How perfect (in your own eyes) are you? How many of your ambitions have you achieved and how many are you actively working towards? How clear are you about your purpose in life?

When we begin the work of personal development, we must think critically about ourselves. We celebrate the areas that are on-point, but we confront the areas that are in opposition to our ideal – or God-ordained – self. To do this, we must resist the temptation to ignore what we don't like about our present selves, because doing so will only give us temporary relief. In the long-run, ignoring the reality of your real-self will only cause more and more dissatisfaction. The distance between your real-self and your ideal, God-ordained self is the rough terrain that must be conquered before you can fully become the person God created you to be and to fulfill your prophetic calling. Your starting point for personal development is your *real-self,* because no matter what you learn or what skills you gain, you will respond to unexpected obstacles and challenging questions from the viewpoint of your real-self. If your real-self is confident and resilient, you'll respond from an "open and ready to grow" mindset. But, if your real-self is insecure and fragile, your response may be *defensive and protective.* Any efforts to hide that fragile person from the people around you will be futile because if your real-self believes you are a failure, that belief will speak louder than any other outward expression of confidence.

We start at real-self, but the destination is to become our *God-ordained self.* Just who is that? I wish I had an answer for you, but I do not. I will, however, tell you who it is not. It's not a perfect, flawless person who effortlessly and blissfully progresses through life's happenings. No one is perfect. When sin entered the Earth, it took away all possibility of us ever being perfect humans. The only perfect human to have ever walked the Earth was Jesus the Christ, so *do not allow your sense of self-worth to abide in your own ability to be perfect (I call this artificial self-worth).* Likewise, do not base your self-worth on how other people *respond* to your perfections, which is flattery, and imperfections. If you actually possessed the ability to be perfect, you would never sin. In the book of 1 John, we see a letter written to Christians and Christian leaders, most likely from Apostle John, saying, "If we say that we have no sin, we are deceiving ourselves and the truth is not in us" (1 John 1:8). And, King Solomon said, "Indeed, there is not a righteous man on earth who continually does good and who never sins" (Ecclesiastes 7:20).

In Mathew 5:48, when Jesus said to us, "Be ye perfect, as your heavenly Father is perfect," He was not saying for us to never make a mistake, never fail, and never error. That interpretation is out of context. Jesus was actually commanding us to not only be kind and loving to our friends, but moreover to expressively show the agape love of the Father to our enemies (see Mathew 5:43-48 and Commandment # 7). Perfectionism is not of God. Anyone whose confidence relies on not making mistakes will find himself living out one or more of these realities:

- Being prideful, arrogant and self-idolizing
- Stuck in a rut and immobile

- Moving forward in life, but in an un-
  healthy and ultimately abusive manner
  (you will abuse yourself and others)

This mindset of artificial self-worth and
perfectionism will strip you of your joy and prevent you from experiencing the fullness of God's
Holy Spirit. King David said, "Lord, who may
abide in Your tent? Who may dwell on Your holy
hill? He who walks with integrity, and works
righteousness, and *speaks truth in his heart*"
(Psalm 15:1-2).

Be confident of this very thing, that He
who began a good work in you will perfect it,
that is ... develop it, until the day of Christ Jesus
(Philippians 1:6). As a follower of Christ, the
Lord will work on developing and perfecting you
for the rest of your life. When you are fully yielded, you will experience noticeable growth, but
not perfection, while growing into your ideal,
God-ordained self.

Once you overcome the need to be perfect, you can really work on growing into your God-ordained self. You should begin with commandment # 12, which is: desire to have the character of God and to live righteously **more than you want anything else in the world**. Matthew 6:33 says it this way, "But seek first His kingdom and His righteousness, and all these things will be added to you."

The next step is very important and it is to follow commandment #33, which is simply to *obey God*. You don't have to understand everything He tells you to do, like it or even agree with it, but you have to have a willingness to simply o-b-e-y Him. Sometimes, obedience is hard because your experiences, life history, and the carnal desires of your real-self will really put up a fight. After all... *you know yourself and God knows your heart*; right? Dear friend, please trust me, you will ALWAYS be better off and get further along when you just obey God.

Finally, with self-development in mind, get even more introspective with yourself and follow commandment #13: Correct your own shortcomings before you tell other people about theirs (Matthew 7:1-6), and don't forsake commandment #28: Before you pray for your own needs, forgive anyone you're holding a grudge against (Mark 11:25-26). The responsibility of being the living gospel all starts with you! When you believe you're seeing a "speck in your brother's eye," your first reaction should be to check yourself first. You may have the same issue working in you. Oftentimes, you cannot see your own shortcomings the way you should see them or you make exceptions and excuses for yourself, generally without even giving it much thought. You do this because you are innately sensitive to your own history, you believe your motives are good so your actions are excusable, or you just don't see the error in yourself. Sometimes the spirit of pride has you in a state of self-deception, and this fallacious way of seeing yourself is one of Satan's best tools for keeping God's children from showing agape love as He commanded, from coming into your God-ordained self, and from advancing the Kingdom. You cannot fully do these things when you're walking in darkness. Jesus said:

"Your eye is a lamp that provides light for your body. When your eye is good, your whole body is filled with light. But when it is bad, your body is filled with darkness. Make sure that the light you think you have is not actually darkness. **If you are filled with light, with no dark corners**, *then your whole life will be radiant, as though a floodlight were filling you with light"* *(Luke 11:34-36 NLT).*

Even the smallest dark corner is a threat to your Kingdom calling and your living witness to others. Work on who you are with your spouse, children, parents, fellow believers, co-workers, colleagues, friends, neighbors, retail customer service attendees, business partners, and so on. Everyone you interact with should observe and come under the influence of Kingdom principals when they know you. 1 Peter 2:12 says, "Be careful how you behave among your unsaved neighbors; for then, *even if* they are suspicious of you and talk against you, they will end up praising God for your good works when Christ returns" (TLB).

Pray and ask God to show you your soul. He knows all of your dark corners. Be honest with Him and bare your whole heart. There is no secret place in Heaven or on Earth where He cannot see you. Give time to prayer, to the dialog of prayer, to meditation, and to praying in the Spirit. Prayer is the key to freeing the soul because through prayer, the Holy Spirit can work deep in those dark corners that you otherwise would not give up. In order for your prayers not to be hindered, you must obey commandment #28: before you pray for your own needs, if you have anything against someone, forgive them (Mark 11:25-26). Forgiveness is a simple concept, but can be emotionally challenging. You can ease the difficulty of forgiveness by realizing that forgiveness is for *you*, and it does not require a response, acknowledgment, nor acceptance from the other person. Forgiveness is an extending of compassion and mercy (commandment #29) by reason of agape love. This is Kingdom advancement.

Chapter 7

To Church Leaders – Our Job is To Develop People

I was having dinner with a dear friend who I grew up with in church. She's a few years younger than me so, at some point in our relationship, I transitioned into an adult leadership role in the church while she continued as a youth. Our perceptions of *church life* began to differ as I learned new, not so healthy, ways of doing church work. It's not that these ways were inherently wrong, as I later learned, they were simply out-of-balance and did not prepare regular attendees for life outside of church. My friend said to me, "You know... I love how we grew up, but I hate the fact that no one ever taught us life skills." I attempted to argue the point that we did teach life skills, but my argument was quickly trumped by her list of life experiences, some almost tragic, that she had to learn how to handle by drawing from resources outside of the church. This is because we simply did not have anything to offer her. Many millennials have expressed similar findings about a hierarchical church, as they call it, with "a do as I say, don't worry about what I do" attitude coming from leadership. Further, I've encountered countless baby boomers who feel like the church they gave so much time, sweat and money to did not help them understand how to grow and develop personally nor professionally. Consequentially, when some of life's toughest moments hit, many felt isolated and ignored. They weren't taught financial education (they were only taught to give). They weren't taught health & nutrition (they were only taught to pray for healing). They weren't taught how to maximize their time (they were taught how and when to come to church). They weren't taught how to handle grief and loss (they were only taught to pray through it and keep busy). There is a great deal of resentment towards the church and it's evident by the decline in church membership and attendance. Consider these statistics provided by the Pew Research Center[1] in 2015:

- Between 2007 and 2014, the Christian population fell from 78.4% to 70.6% and non-Christian faiths grew by 1.2%.

- Between 2007 and 2014, the number of atheist, agnostics or "nothing in particular" grew from 16.1% to 22.8%.

- Mainstream Protestant and Evangelicals experienced the greatest decline, and the black church generally remained flat with only a minor loss of .4%.

- Nearly one-in-five marriages in 2010 included one person who was a Christian and one person who was not.

- Roughly 34-36% of Millennials are less connected with the Christian church than previous generations.

I don't believe these declining numbers exist because people don't want God. In fact, many have said it is their personal experience with the power of God that has kept them going when "organized religion" let them down. These are their words, not mine.

I address this chapter to church leaders, not because I want to bring shame or to cause offense. I'm writing to help ministry leaders bring healing to a tottering institution. As leaders, our number one job is to develop people who: (1) fully understand discipleship and the vision for Kingdom advancement, (2) know their roles in carrying out Kingdom responsibilities, and (3) are developed personally and spiritually enough to be influential at home, in the community, in the workplace, as well as in the connected network of local church assemblies.

Jesus, the Christ, said the gates of hell would never prevail against the Church that is built upon Him as the Rock. He and He alone is the foundation of the Church that hell can never defeat (Matthew 16:18). If you build your local body on the foundational teaching and truth of Jesus, it will accomplish the purpose God called it to fulfill. It cannot lose. It's simply impossible.

Secondly, Jesus said, "See to it that no one misleads you. For many will come in My name, saying, 'I am the Christ,' and [they] **will mislead many**...Then they will deliver you to tribulation, and will kill you, and you will be hated by all nations because of My name. At that time **many will fall away** and will betray one another and hate one another. Many false prophets will arise and [performing great signs and wonders] **will mislead many**...But the one who endures to the end, he will be saved" (Matthew 24:4-14, 24).

A not-so-welcomed outcome of this scriptural truth is this: the local church that continues teaching the true gospel of the Kingdom and places emphasis on making disciples may ultimately decrease in size. We cannot become so disheartened by decreasing numbers that we compromise the great commission, neither can we be proponents of faulty prophetics in order to keep church attendees engaged.

Thirdly, when Jesus, being confronted by a Talmid Chacham (an expert in Jewish law), was asked how He could inherit eternal life, He referred the expert back to the law he knew so well, saying, "We're commanded to love our neighbor as our self." The Talmid Chacham then asked, "Who is my neighbor?" To that, Jesus told the parable of the Good Samaritan who, upon seeing a man beat-up, robbed, left for dead on the side of the road, and then being passed over by two religious men, cleaned and soothed up his wounds. He then bandaged him up, physically carried him to the nearest inn, paid for his lodging, stayed with him all night, and then made arrangements with the innkeeper to continue caring for this stranger on his (that is the Samaritan's) good credit. Point number three is that the mission of Kingdom advancement needs every follower of Christ to have the mindset, resources and abilities to compassionately serve the needs of our community. This is a leadership role that does not wait for *someone* to do something. Followers of Christ must be able to see a need, discern the integrity of it, and then wisely take the appropriate action.

As a pastor and leader in today's church, I understand the challenges in leading a body of believers into this type of Kingdom responsibility. Firstly, because so many people come to church with a consumer's mentality, they may not respond very favorably to this type of accountability. Think about every member in your congregation. What would it take for you to convince every one of them to intentionally participate in such Kingdom advancement activities on an on-going basis? Secondly, consider the extensive amount of motivational planning, deliberate teaching, and personal involvement it would take to develop this type of local body. Our roles as ministry leaders would need to expand greatly in order to meet this challenge. Even our teaching of the Bible would change to be more along the pattern of Jesus' style of didactic discourse. Jesus knew what the disciples would face when He sent them out into the world, so He taught them using dialogues, debates and parables. This means the discussions were very interactive. Most ministry leaders shy away from these types of teaching methods because they fear they'll lose control. Some don't do it because they might not be able to answer the varying questions and comments that arise. Others simply have never considered it because of church traditions, the size of their congregations, or their objection to small-study groups. In most cases, the primary rationale is so that the ministry leader feels a sense of control, or as some would call it, "unity." What would happen if congregants started asking too many questions? Are not questions the foundation of learning and discovery? Questioning is what separates the actively engaged learner from the passive one. The actively engaged learner is the one who will take independent ownership of his/her journey into a relationship with Christ, and therefore, may not be as dependent on the ministry leader as some others. We mustn't fear their independence, but rather, help support their growth in a way that emphasizes a personal relationship with Christ and an interdependent relationship with the body of Christ. We cannot comfortably do this if we're walking in fear or insecurity.

When a ministry leader suffers from fear and/or insecurity, it prevents him/her from exercising the right balance between a "teachable moment" and "behavioral discipline," which ultimately sabotages growth for everyone involved. Another tendency of an insecure ministry leader is to over-protect congregants. Leaders who have a caring shepherd's heart sometimes find it much easier to *over-protect* their members than it is to *teach them* and hold them accountable until transformation happens. Jesus spent an incredible amount of time teaching His disciples, developing character in them and preparing them to carry on the work of Kingdom advancement in His absence. He taught them first to be disciples and second, to go out as ministers advancing the Kingdom. The unfortunate outcome of underdeveloped believers is a weak local church whose members generally struggle to influence others. Weak local churches cannot meet the God-ordained mandate for His universal Church. Jesus Christ was so keen on the fact that believers would need all that He had and more in order to be **in the world doing His work** that He prayed:

"Father, the hour has come; glorify Your Son, that the Son may glorify You... I glorified You on the earth, having accomplished the work which You have given Me to do... I have manifested Your name to the men whom You gave Me out of the world; they were Yours and You gave them to Me, and they have kept Your word... Now they have come to know that everything You have given Me is from You; for the words which You gave Me I have given to them; and they received them... I am no longer in the world; and yet they themselves are in the world, and I come to You. Holy Father, keep them in Your name...While I was with them, I

was keeping them in Your name... But now I come to You... **I do not ask You to take them out of the world, but to keep them** *from the evil one. They are not of the world, even as I am not of the world. Sanctify them in the truth; Your word is truth... I do not ask on behalf of these alone, but for those also who believe in Me through their word...that they may all be one" (John 17).*

Leaders, we must get back to developing people to do the work of Christ. Jesus accomplished what God instructed Him to do while in the Earth, and He will return in the future to put the final closure on it. In the meantime, we, the local church and all of our covenant keeping members, are to continue working as Christ commanded us to do. Jesus said, "Greater works will you do...." In order for believers to do greater works, we have to develop them to have a greater works mentality - a transformational way of thinking that will transcend across every area of life. When people see us *in the world,* they should see the character and wholeness of

Christ. What if we intentionally taught congregants how to distinguish the fruit of a false prophet from the fruit of a true prophet, especially since both have the power to work miracles, signs and wonders? What if we taught the people charged to our care to grow, not only in the things of the church, but also in their occupations, in financial health, and in their ability to see a problem in their communities and then produce a creative solution for it?

If we are going to be a mature local church and a beacon of light in our communities, we have to be committed to developing people more than we are to developing programs and organizations, as these things will naturally flow out of well-developed believers.

What is the responsibility of the ministry leader? 1 Peter 5:1-4 (NLT) says:

"And now, a word to you who are elders in the churches... As a fellow elder, I appeal to you: Care for the flock that God has entrusted to you.

Watch over it willingly, not grudgingly—not for what you will get out of it, but because you are eager to serve God. Don't lord it over the people assigned to your care, but lead them by your own good example. And when the Great Shepherd appears, you will receive a crown of never-ending glory and honor."

In this passage, I see four instructions: (1) care for them, (2) watch over them, (3) do not lord over them, and (4) lead them by example. If we do these four things from Christ-centered motives, those who remain in our care will mature and develop according to God's will for their lives. Our leadership should help them reach their God-ordained selves, wherein they discover how God wants to use their lives to advance His Kingdom culture in the Earth.

As ministry leaders, we must remember that a person will never reach his fullest potential when his gifts, talents, and personality traits have not been developed. Our watchful care and leadership should prepare our congregants to excel both in the church and in the world. In John 10:7-10, Jesus Christ said, "I am the door of the sheep...by me if any man enters in, he shall be saved, and shall go in and out, and find pasture...I have come that they might have life, and that they might have [it] more abundantly."

We know Jesus was not talking about four-legged animals in this passage; He was talking about people. He said His people would be able to (1) safely go in and out, (2) find pasture, and (3) they would be able to live their lives more abundantly. The ability to go in and out means the sheep know how to go, where to go, where not to go, how to get along with others in the society where they go, how to communicate to get results, when to stand up for themselves, when to let a situation go without argument, and are not afraid to do any of these things with boldness. To find pasture means that the people know how to access all supplies and resources needed for a prosperous life, and can obtain those supplies and resources as needed. To live life more abundantly means, not only does the sheep obtain the supplies and resources needed for an ordinary life, but additionally obtains all that is needed for an extraordinary life. It means they have more than enough — more than what is common among men.

An undeveloped/underdeveloped person will struggle to obtain these promises and may even begin feeling as if they're failing God. I don't want any of my congregants feeling this type of lowness, and I'm sure you don't either. We have to consider how we (the ministry leaders) need to change and develop so we can lead congregants through this type of transformation as well. It starts with leadership first.

Chapter 8

Get The 'Christ Perspective' on Leadership

Leadership; taking the lead in the task or mission you've been given.

It is true that we've all been given a mission to accomplish because everything God made has a purpose to serve. Back in the summer of 2015, I attempted to start my very first barrel garden, and for a city girl like me, it was a real experience. I learned so much about plant life and gained invaluable allegorical insights on the human experience while trying to produce a small harvest of vegetables. I attempted to grow lettuce, carrots, cucumbers and bell peppers, learning day by day what to expect. Early on, when I first planted my cucumbers, I chopped down my rose bush thinking it served no purpose other than aesthetics. You see, I thought I needed the space for my vegetables. As I progressed through the various growth stages of my garden, I soon learned that cucumbers bloom flowers, and in order for the flower to transform into a cucumber, it needed bees to stop by and pollinate them. My cucumber flowers kept blooming, dying and falling off because, as it turned out, bees are not naturally attracted to cucumber flowers. I asked my local Master Gardener for help, and she said, "You need a *rose bush* or some nasturtiums nearby the cucumbers to attract the bees." I had underestimated the usefulness of my rose bush. In the roses was the potential to attract bees, which would have served the purpose of helping me produce cucumbers. Everything God made has a purpose.

I believe this is a viewpoint into Christ's perspective on leadership. Everyone God made has a purpose and a mission, and each of us must take the lead on that given mission. From this perspective, we are all born with a call to leadership.[1] This role is not leadership *over* people, but rather leadership to carry out a mission and to make sure it is completed. God, in His authorship of leadership, created us in His image and immediately told us to "have *dominion* over...every living *thing* that moves on the earth" (Genesis 1:28). Dominion is a leadership position; it's over *things,* and not necessarily over people. An attempt to usurp dominion over another person will only lead to a tumultuous relationship of resentment.

God placed certain natural instincts in every living thing. He gave man, having been created in the express likeness of God, the ability to use every other living thing to his advantage for the purpose of maintaining and multiplying a strong human race for His glory. God also tasked man with the responsibility of tilling, dressing and keeping the Garden of Eden. Adam and Eve were to take the lead on ensuring man's food source never ran out. They were to work together, not in competition, nor was one to take supremacy over the other. Right from the start, God gave them leadership and responsibility over *the cause* of multiplying what He started. This was 'Mission Kingdom Advancement,' day number one. Even though sin separated us from our original position of dominion, the regenerative work of Christ on the cross afforded each of us the opportunity to reconcile with God and reclaim our rightful place. The problem is, too many of us (believers) don't really want it. We want the authority and the luxury of dominion, but we do not want the responsibility of it. Responsibility means w-o-r-k. Your purpose is your work.

Because sin is in the world, we must now carry out our work/purpose in a world where Satan is king and where the carnality in our own soul fights against us. None of us are exempt from the struggle of keeping our carnal minds aligned with the will of God. Consider Matthew 4:8-11:

"Again, the devil took Him (Jesus) to a very high mountain and showed Him all the kingdoms of the world and their glory; and he said to Him, "All these things I will give You, if You fall down and worship me." Then Jesus said to him, "Go, Satan! For it is written, 'You shall worship the Lord your God, and serve Him only.'" Then the devil left Him; and behold, angels came and began to minister to Him."

Note what happened here:

(1) Just when Christ was to begin the most crucial (and painful) part of His earthly work, Satan presented Him with the option to exchange *fighting to unleash the Kingdom of Heaven* for the 'gift' of owning all the *kingdoms of this world*.

(2) We can deduce that Satan rules the kingdoms of this world, otherwise he could not have offered to give them to Jesus.

(3) Jesus Christ understood that when Satan said, "Fall down and worship me," he was

actually asking Him to dethrone God as the King of kings.

(4) When Jesus was resolute to only worship AND serve the Lord, He knew that serving meant working and performing in somewhat of a slave-like manner, for no other reason but to glorify God.

(5) The fight between Jesus and Satan was so tough that angels had to come minister to Him to restore His strength.

If you think for one minute that Satan does not or will not approach you and me in the same way when it comes to working out our purpose, you are sadly mistaken and no doubt are already in a state of compromise. Likewise, if you think taking the lead in the work God has given you to do means the mission will be easy and trouble-free, you're going to be disappointed in true Kingdom advancement. Because of this, you may find yourself looking for some other feel-good alternative that *appears* to have a Kingdom focus (as expressed in note #1 above).

Remember our definition of Kingdom advancement? *Intentionally taking the character of God, which you noticeably carry once you've been redeemed and transformed by Christ, to those who do not live by it, and doing so in such a way that your influence gradually shifts their lifestyle practices and behaviors.* The work or purpose God has placed in you to do is the *vehicle for* Kingdom advancement, but the way in which you carry it out releases the influential Kingdom character of God everywhere that vehicle takes you. This is why we need to memorize, memorialize, characterize, and strategize our life's work in accordance with the 35 commandments of Christ that we discussed in chapter three. Real Kingdom advancement can only happen when believers excel in living out Christ's commandments to every people and nation on the Earth.

Jesus Christ took 12 ordinary, perhaps undervalued men who had *proven* they could be His disciples, and He taught them His commandments, commissioned them for their work, and then sent them two-by-two out to do the work. Notice Jesus did not assign a team captain because He did not need to. Why? Because of *true discipleship*. In biblical times, a person was not a disciple until he, as the student, was able to do what the teacher did. A disciple learned the ways of the teacher so much so that he would be an imitator of him, whether in his presence or not. From a Hebraic perspective, the disciple essentially became the same person as the teacher (the Master/Rabbi)[2]. The goal of discipleship was not to teach man to be a follower, but rather to lead *as* a Master/Rabbi. Oh how strong the Christian church would be if we emphasized developing congregants to lead like Christ Jesus, and not merely to be followers of our ministry. Help us Lord.

After a night of fervent prayer, Jesus chose from His many disciples the 12 who would unitedly take the lead (or go first) in the Apostolic Kingdom advancement. He did not go looking for the top talents; He didn't sort out those who were full of charisma, nor did He select people who already had an entourage of followers. He prayed all night and then chose 12 proven men from the multitude of disciples to become the apostles.

"It was at this time that He went off to the mountain to pray, and He spent the whole night in prayer to God. And when day came, He called His disciples to Him and chose twelve of them, whom He also named as apostles: Simon, whom He also named Peter, and Andrew his brother; and James and John; and Philip and Bartholomew; and Matthew and Thomas; James the son of Alphaeus, and Simon who was called the Zealot; Judas the son of James, and Judas Iscariot, who became a traitor" (Matthew 10:12-16).

Apostle Paul eventually took what man would call a 'chief leadership role' in expanding God's Kingdom on Earth, but not because he was initially appointed to be over anyone. Paul's level of commitment coupled with the extreme transformation in his thinking and his belief system catapulted him into a position that no devil in hell or human on Earth could ever take from him. However, if Apostle Paul had not fully committed to: 1) becoming a person very different from the one he was raised and groomed to be, and 2) becoming a person who would willingly take apostolic orders from the words and work of Christ, he most certainly would not have completed the work God created him to do. God would have chosen another transformed, willing, and capable person to do His work. The apostolic never stops because of human negligence.

True discipleship will cost you - all of you. True discipleship proceeds Apostolic Kingdom advancement, because Kingdom advancement is character first, with the work coming second. Jesus' leadership pattern produced proven disciples first, and then it launched delegated leaders second. If we're going to be effective for the Kingdom, you and I must get this order right. And, even while we're carrying out the work, we must continually meditate on the teachings of

Christ so that we always maintain our stance as disciples or, in other words, imitators of Christ. We should be carrying this apostolic power into every corner of the Earth, in everything we do, and to every life we touch.

Yes, you were born purposed for leadership, but you only *become* that leader when you make the individual changes needed to attain it. This means taking the lead over your character development as well as your given assignment, and doing so in such a way that creates space and opportunities for companions to come along with you, alongside of you, and to come after you. You're paving new pathways and finding new avenues for Kingdom expansion. Kingdom advancement is not about exciting the church; it's about *you* influencing the world with the leadership-ability of our God and King.

Chapter 9

Transform

We sing, talk, and preach about living transformed lives but, in truth, transformation isn't an outward work. Transformation takes place in the mind, then in the heart, and finally, it shows up in our outward actions. It is marked by a turning point: a place or position in your mind where you realize that unless you make a real change, the vision for your future will die.

I will never forget the tragedy of September 11, 2001, when 19 Al-Qaeda terrorists hijacked four airliners and carried out the infamous suicide attacks against the United States. Two planes were flown into the World Trade Center towers, one was flown into the Pentagon, and the fourth plane crashed in a field in Pennsylvania, missing its intended target because alerted passengers fought back. Among the more than 6000 lives lost as a result of 9/11 were: 2,606 in the World Trade Center, 125 at the Pentagon, 356 airline passengers, and 411 emergency workers. Nearly 18,000 people suffered from illnesses and fatal diseases as a result of toxic carcinogens polluting the airways after the attack.[1] Over 3,000 children lost a parent,[2] and it's estimated that nearly 84,000 New Yorkers became unemployed[3] all as a result of this one act. Overnight, the vision of one man, carried out by the works of 19, transformed the World Trade Center towers into dust, and changed the lives of most Americans forever.

What if this horrible, life-transforming event left everyone so despondent and hopeless that we just left ground zero in a pile of toxic dust? What if the brokenness of yesterday - or in this case, of September 11th – completely depleted us of having vision for a better, more meaningful future? No such thing happened at the ground zero site of 9/11. Fourteen years later, the rebuilding of the World Trade Center and the revival of Lower Manhattan was almost complete. It's branding included phrases such as, "What tomorrow looks like"[4], "Reaching new heights," "Bigger. Bolder. Better than ever," and "A neighborhood reborn." The transformed region has taller, more architecturally complex and beautifully designed buildings that are filled with endless amenities, and thoughtfully considered memorials for all to see and experience. This transformation would not have been possible if someone did not have a vision and was willing to see it through. Transformation is a healthy survival mechanism that says, *I refuse to lose my God-ordained self to my current situation.* It's telling yourself, *Yes, I do have a vision for my life, and I will transform so I can attain it.*

Many Christians never get to the place of living transformed by the renewing of their minds for at least one of these five reasons:

1. We don't understand that transformation and repentance work hand-in-hand.

2. We don't accept that this level of transformation is required of us.

3. We fail to assess our choices all throughout the day.

4. We're not disciplined enough to break ourselves from old habits and old ways of thinking so we can implement new ones.

5. Our lack of vision and/or discipline hinders us from taking intentional leadership over our own life.

Transformation and Repentance Work Hand-in-Hand

When Jesus, the Messiah, preached, "Repent!" He was not saying "apologize," nor was He imploring us "to be sorry" for our sins. This narrow understanding of the word *repent* is from an Old Testament transliteration of the Hebrew word *nacham*. Until Christ became the ultimate sacrifice for our sins, being apologetic, helpless sinners was our only alternative. Jesus came to the Earth to implement a transformational reconciliatory plan that gave us access to God's original plan for His creation. Thus, "repent," when it came from Jesus' mouth, was *metanoeō* which means: "to change one's mind for better, to heartily amend with abhorrence of one's past sins, and to think differently."

Transformation is a Requirement

The intention and purpose of repenting must not be taken lightly. It is the moment in time of your turning point. *Repent* is the very second when you wholeheartedly decide it's time to transform, and that means it's time to renew your mind. At that moment, the service of renewing your mind must begin. You cannot "prove" that you've accepted God's will until you commit to transforming.

*Romans 12:1-2 says: "Therefore I urge you, brethren, by the mercies of God, to present your bodies a living and holy sacrifice, acceptable to God, which is your spiritual service of worship. And do not be conformed to this world, **but be transformed by the renewing of your mind, so***

that you may prove what the will of God is, *that which is good and acceptable and perfect."*

Conforming requires very little effort, no vision, and is a 'follower's' mentality. Society expects you to conform, and to not conform means you'll be labeled and criticized. Conforming means you get to stick with the crowd and *go with the flow*. It makes you buy into the falsehood of: "if everyone is doing it, it must be right." Conforming makes you more acceptable because you *look* like a team-player, and it relieves you of the responsibility of pointing out a different, perhaps more righteous, path.

The scripture says, "Be not conformed to this world..." The world and all of its systems work hard to convince us that something is *right*, when we know it is wrong as soon as we consult the law of the Lord that's in our hearts and minds. The comfort of social conformity seeks to overthrow the eternal protection of knowledge. It does not matter how many church services, conferences, workshops, classes, seminars, or mentoring events you attend, until you take action in accordance with Godly knowledge, you will continue in societal conformity.

Transformation doesn't happen in your body; it happens in your mind, filters through your heart and then it displays outwardly through your body. You're transformed by the renewing of the mind, not by the confession of your lips. Confession, however, helps your faith because faith comes by hearing.

Another important factor in achieving a transformed life is healing of the heart. The heart needs to be healed from disappointments, rejection, abandonment, life tragedies, childhood issues, and manipulation. All of these have most likely shaped a heart that does not trust and cannot see truth as it should. Strongholds take root in the mind and prevent it from being renewed. Healing the heart and renewing the mind are tough processes, but your confessions will help you maintain faith while you work through it.

Assessing Your Choices

Renewing the mind is not about focusing on sin; it's a cognitive brain function in which you constantly assess your daily customs, practices and habits, and you measure each one against the law of the Lord. Hebrews 10:10-11, 14-16 says:

By this will we have been sanctified through the offering of the body of Jesus Christ once for all. Every priest stands daily ministering and offering time after time the same sacrifices, which can never take away sins. For by one offering He has perfected for all time those who are sanctified. And the Holy Spirit also testifies to us; for after saying: "This is the covenant that I will make with them, 'after those days, says the Lord: I will put My laws upon their heart, And on their mind I will write them.'"

The Lord said He would put His law on the hearts and in the minds of all who willingly surrendered to the call of transformation. The heart and the mind are where decisions are made. God knows we need His law to be present every time we're deciding what to think and do about any given situation. Repentance commits you to changing your mind and your way of thinking, so that the decisions you make about your life now are quite different than they were before. You're committing to allow God's law to guide and challenge your choices in ways that may go against your own natural desires. But as we make doing His will our priority, transformation and full repentance happens.

What is the Law of the Lord? As theologians grapple with trying to make a distinction between the Law of the Lord vs. the Law of Moses, I'll simply sum it up using the words of Christ. In Matthew 22:35-40 He expressed:

- "'You shall love the Lord your God with all your heart, and with all your soul, and with all your mind.' **This is the great and foremost commandment**. The second is like it, 'You shall love your neighbor as yourself.' **On these two commandments depend the whole Law** and the Prophets."

In Matthew 23:23 He explained that:

- Justice, mercy and faithfulness are weighty provisions of the Law of the Lord.

In Matthew 23:28 He implied that:

- The Law of the Lord is to be applied first-ly as an **inward** work .

And in Mark 3:3-5 He demonstrated that:

- The Law of the Lord would not impede restoration.

  How blessed are those whose way
  is blameless, who walk in the law
  of the Lord.

  How blessed are those who observe His testimonies, who seek
  Him with all their heart. They also
  do no unrighteousness; they walk
  in His ways.

Psalm 119:1-3

Breaking Old Habits and Forming New Ones

Habits are recurring behaviors we do subconsciously because, at some point in our youth and/or adult lives, we consciously did them repetitively. Once we found that the behavior brought comfort or pleasure whenever a certain thing happened, we continued allowing it to be the response to certain trigger points. There are good habits, which serve to protect us from harm, and there are bad habits, which lead to injury and grief. Anyone who is going to transform his life by renewing the mind must become more conscientious of his habits. This means allowing the Holy Spirit to bring those harmful habits from your subconscious, fossilized memory into your conscious, working memory. A fossilized mind isn't pliable enough to be renewed. This is why a healthy, Spirit-led prayer life is key. Prayer heals hearts, breaks the power of mental strongholds, and helps you access those God-given dreams and visions.

Once you're able to identify your harmful habits, what can you do to break them? Breaking old habits and forming new ones is truly a process, and no one will ever be an overnight sensation at it. According to psychologist Dr. Art Markman[5], habits are memories that work automatically in effort to please you right now; they're mostly concerned about short-term, quick-fixes. What this means is actions performed out of habit generally will not consider long-term benefits or consequences. In the brain (or mind), which is your decision making hotspot, are two systems: the "go system" and the "stop system." The "go system" goes to work first to immediately fulfill your need or want without giving time for reason or choice. The "stop system" comes along right after to help you weigh out or inhibit the behavior you're about to do. In order to break an old habit, Dr. Markman suggests that instead of focusing on breaking a bad habit, give more thought to making the good habit easier and more enjoyable to do.

I appreciate Dr. Markman's clinical advice, and believe it's definitely helpful for changing physical habits - for example, if you want to break the habit of drinking soda pop, you could focus on how to make healthy beverages more flavorful and interesting. Taming bad soulish habits, however, will require a different approach. To break bad soulish habits, for example, if you're habitually passive-aggressive, have a quick temper, or hide behind make-believe stories, you'll have to identify the stronghold in your life, get to the root cause, and give the Lord free reign to walk you through the healing process. I love the way author and Bible teacher, Beth Moore, in her book *Breaking Free,* makes this point:

"A stronghold could be anything from compulsive eating to paranoia, from bitterness to obsessive love. No matter what it may be, all strongholds have one thing in common: Satan is fueling the mental tank with deception to keep the stronghold running... If you know a stronghold exists somewhere in your life, but you cannot identi-

fy the lies, you are still captive...Please ask God to drop the scales from your eyes and help you see! 'Then you will know the truth, and the truth will set you free.'"[6]

Once you've identified the habits that need to be eliminated, and confronted the lies that fuel them, a continued healthy life of prayer, meditation, and persistent application of God's Word will give you what's needed to renew your mind and form new habits. Start with the list of 35 commandments in chapter 4, and then add the good habits found in the 10 passages of scripture below:

1. Proverbs 8:34-36 - Blessed is the man who listens to me (wisdom), Watching *daily* at my gates, waiting at my doorposts. For he who finds me (wisdom) finds life and obtains favor from the Lord. But he who sins against me (wisdom) injures himself; All those who hate me (wisdom) love death.

2. Proverbs 23:17 - Do not let your heart envy sinners, but live in the fear of the Lord *always.*

3. Proverbs 29:11 - A fool *always* loses his temper, but a wise man holds it back.

4. Acts 24:16 - In view of this, I also do my best to maintain *always* a blameless conscience both before God and before men.

5. 2 Corinthians 15:58 - Therefore, my beloved brethren, be steadfast, immovable, *always* abounding in the work of the Lord.

6. 2 Corinthians 5:6-8 Therefore, being *always* of good courage, and knowing that while we are at home in the body we are absent from the Lord— for we walk by faith, not by sight— we are of good courage.

7. Philippians 2:12 - So then, my beloved, just as you have *always* obeyed, not as in

my presence only, but now much more in my absence, work out your salvation with fear and trembling.

8. Philippians 4:4 - Rejoice in the Lord *always*; again I will say, rejoice!

9. Colossians 4:6 - Let your speech *always* be with grace, as though seasoned with salt, so that you will know how you should respond to each person.

10. 1 Thessalonians 5:15-16 - See that no one repays another with evil for evil, but *always* seek after that which is good for one another and for all people. Rejoice *always.*

Taking the Lead Over Your Own Self

The late Dr. Myles Munroe published several videotaped teachings in a series called *The Leading Edge Leadership Show*. The purpose of the teaching series is to "**transform followers into leaders,**" stating that every believer is born with the capacity to lead. He begins the series by stating three basic principles you must know in order to become the leader God ordained you to be. He says:

"First of all, you must believe that you were born with the capacity to influence other people and the world. Secondly, you must believe that you possess the potential and the ability to influence the world with your gifts. Thirdly, you must believe that you were created by God and born in this generation because whatever you have, your generation needs. That means you are significant to the world."[7]

One of the reasons we fail to transform is because we lack the vision and/or discipline needed to take intentional leadership over our own lives. I was leading a meeting with a few of our church members one day; we were trying to discover more ways a small church like ours could make a bigger impact in our community. Someone said, "We could make a bigger difference if *someone* would empower us." To that I responded, "If *someone* empowers us, that same someone can *unempower* us at any time."

The sense of empowerment to pursue the vision for your life is a power that must come from within. As children of God, the scriptures continually inform us of who and what that power source is. Consider these passages:

1. John 14:17 - ...The Spirit of truth, whom the world cannot receive, because it does not see Him or know Him, but you know Him because He abides *with you and will be in you.*

2. Romans 8:11- He who raised Christ Jesus from the dead will also give life to your mortal bodies through His Spirit who *dwells in you.*

3. 1 Corinthians 1:4-6 - ...I thank my God always concerning you for the grace of God which was *given you in* Christ Jesus, that in everything *you were enriched* in Him, in all speech and all knowledge, even as the testimony concerning Christ was *confirmed in you*, so that you are not lacking in any gift...

4. 1 Corinthians 3:16 - Do you not know that you are a temple of God and that the Spirit of God *dwells in you*?

5. Philippians 1:6 - For I am confident of this very thing, that He who began a *good work in you* will perfect it until the day of Christ Jesus.

6. Philippians 2:13 - for it is God who is *at work in you*, both to will and to work for His good pleasure.

7. Colossians 1:27 - ...God willed to make known what is the riches of the glory of this mystery among the Gentiles, which is *Christ in you*, the hope of glory.

8. 2 Thessalonians 1:11-12 - To this end also we pray for you always, that our God will count you worthy of your calling, and fulfill every desire for goodness and the work of faith with power, so that the name of our *Lord Jesus will be glorified in you*, and you in Him, according to the

grace of our God and the Lord Jesus Christ.

9. 2 Timothy 1:14 - Guard, through the *Holy Spirit who dwells in us*, the treasure which has been *entrusted to you.*

Believe this: the power to lead is in you! The challenge, however, is understanding what this really means. The world and all its systems, have convinced us that leadership is a dominating, authoritarian role over people. Herein lies the problem, and it's a problem that covers a wide spectrum from:

- "I want to lead so I can legitimately have the final say..." to
- "I don't want to lead because I don't want to be responsible for the outcome..." to
- "I'm not interested enough in participating to even care who leads..."

I challenge you to find anywhere in the scriptures where either of these positions is the heart and character of God the Father, the Son or the Holy Ghost. This mentality is anti-kingdom of God.

Dr. David Oyedepo, presiding Bishop of Living Faith Church Worldwide in Ogun State, Nigeria, explains leadership like this:

"Leadership is not about leading people; it's about taking the lead in your field [in a way] that makes men refer to you... It is not occupying a seat; it is accomplishing a feat – an outstanding task. Leadership is taking the lead, not talking the lead... It's not about teaching principles; it's about setting examples... Leadership is about blazing the trail."[8]

I can easily see the leadership process of Jesus Christ in His life on Earth in Dr. Oyedepo's description of leadership. Transformation of ourselves for the Kingdom's sake requires this type of leadership from every believer.

To lead, you must have two visions: (1) a personal vision of your *God-ordained self*, and (2) a vision of the mission God purposed you to carry out - the feat you are to accomplish. When you're committed to these two visions, it will force you to create new habits— habits that work favorably for the convergence of your two visions. Every believer who receives the indwelling of the Holy Ghost should have a vision for his or her life. It was on the day of Pentecost when the Holy Ghost fell on all the believers in the Upper Room, as recorded in Acts chapter 2, that some of the Jews mocked and accused the tongue-talking believers of being drunk. That's when Peter spoke up, prompting everyone to remember the prophetic word of God spoken by the prophet Joel many years prior:

*"'And it shall be in the last days,' God says, 'That I will pour forth of My Spirit **on all mankind**; and your sons and your daughters shall prophesy, and your young men shall see **visions**, And your old men shall dream dreams."*

God is a God of truth and He is looking for vessels of truth to whom He can reveal His strategies. Any follower of Christ who is able to see and understand the visions God reveals should consider it a blessing. In Matthew 13:10-17, Jesus explains this very point to the disciples. The option to see visions is available to every-one, but the ability to see is only open to those whose hearts are not hardened.

The saddest woe of too many people is: "I want something different, but I keep on looking for it amongst my old things wondering where is it?

Until you're clear on your vision, you'll be undisciplined and unsatisfied with life, and in-variably looking to someone else (or to someone else's vision) to give you a sense of value and purpose. Proverbs 29:18 says, "Where there is no vision, the people are unrestrained..." No one can tell you what your vision is, but once you can articulate it, other people can help you plan out the steps to bring it to fruition. You'll begin to see how your manifested vision can be fitly-joined to another believer's vision, working in concert to bringing even more glory to God, our Father. When you prove you're committed to the vision, resources will begin to show up.

Chapter 10

Transformation, Repentance, and the Five Churches Jesus Rebuked

We live in a world in which trendy things can often lead us away from our Kingdom calling. Sometimes, 'what's trending' is counter-productive to our commitment to living transformed lives. This is not a new challenge for the believer. Jesus Christ sent the message of "Repent" to five of the seven local community churches in Asia Minor. Revelatory theologians ascertain that these churches typify all churches of every age since Pentecost, and represent the problems congregations of believers still face today. Thinking of the 'seven spheres of influence,' we can identify the most evident system of influence in each town in which the churches were located. The same systems influence us today. We should therefore hear and obey Christ's call to repentance in the same manner. Let's look at them one-by-one.

Repent and Transform Back to Loving God With All Your Heart, Soul and Mind

Ephesus, a region similar to our modern day New York, was a rich cosmopolitan town. Situated right on the water, it was one of the most important banking, trade, commercial and education centers in the region. Although the people in this city were highly intellectual, immorally sexual and very much into the pagan worship of Artemis and other gods, a small church of Christians thrived there. The challenge these believers faced was that even though they understood the truths of God very well, they did not have a heart after the things of God. Their head knowledge was not enough to keep them, so they fell back into their old ways. Jesus called them to repent, and transform back to loving God with all their hearts, souls and minds.

The dominating spheres in this region were business, education, and religion.

"To the angel of the church in Ephesus write: The One who holds the seven stars in His right hand, the One who walks among the seven golden lampstands, says this: 'I know your deeds and your toil and perseverance, and that you cannot tolerate evil men, and you put to the test those who call themselves apostles, and they are not, and you found them to be false, and you have perseverance and have endured for My name's sake, and have not grown weary. But I have this against you, that you have left your first love. Therefore remember from where you have fallen, and repent and do the deeds you did at first; or else I am coming to you and will remove your lampstand out of its place—unless you repent. Yet this you do have, that you hate the deeds of the Nicolaitans, which I also hate. He who has an ear, let him hear what the Spirit says to the churches. To him who overcomes, I will grant to eat of the tree of life which is in the Paradise of God."

Revelations 2:1-7

Repent and Hold Firmly to Christ's Teachings

Pergamum was a very political city. It was the city where the Roman government resided in all of its glory. Its citizens were oftentimes very intellectual, sophisticated, nymphomaniac, poly-theistic idol worshippers, but the greatest chal-lenge for the Christians who lived there was the expectation of emperor worship. In Pergamum, Roman Emperor Caesar Augustus was wor-shipped and esteemed above every other god. The church at Pergamum had become the com-promising church. Jesus called them to repent and to firmly hold to His teachings.

The dominating spheres in this region were government, education, and media.

"And to the angel of the church in Perga-mum write: The One who has the sharp two-edged sword says this: 'I know where you dwell, where Satan's throne is; and you hold fast My name, and

did not deny My faith even in the days of Antipas,
My witness, My faithful one, who was killed among
you, where Satan dwells. But I have a few things
against you, because you have there some who
hold the teaching of Balaam, who kept teaching
Balak to put a stumbling block before the sons of
Israel, to eat things sacrificed to idols and to com-
mit acts of immorality. So you also have some who
in the same way hold the teaching of the Nicolai-
tans. Therefore repent; or else I am coming to you
quickly, and I will make war against them with
the sword of My mouth. He who has an ear, let
him hear what the Spirit says to the churches. To
him who overcomes, to him I will give some of the
hidden manna, and I will give him a white stone,
and a new name written on the stone which no
one knows but he who receives it.'
Revelations 2:12-17

Repent and Stop Engaging in Seducing Behav-iors and Sexual Immorality

Thyatira, a seemingly insignificant town, had one of the smallest churches, but received the longest letter. In contemporary terms, Thyatira was a major manufacturing town where belonging to a trade labor union and having a strong work ethic was the cultural norm. Each labor union would hold regular "networking events" where members would eat, drink, worship the god(s) most closely associated to their business industry, and would engage in sexual activities as a means to secure business deals. The challenge for the Christian church here was that they tolerated adultery and other immoral behavior and turned a blind eye to the seductive spirit of Jezebel. Jesus promised severe punishment to those who did not turn away from this lifestyle. The dominating spheres in this region were business and arts and entertainment.

"And to the angel of the church in Thyatira write: The Son of God, who has [eyes like a flame of fire, and His feet are like burnished bronze, says this: 'I know your deeds, and your love and faith and service and perseverance, and that your deeds of late are greater than at first. But I have this

against you, that you tolerate the woman Jezebel, who calls herself a prophetess, and she teaches and leads My bond-servants astray so that they commit acts of immorality and eat things sacrificed to idols. I gave her time to repent, and she does not want to repent of her immorality. Behold, I will throw her on a bed of sickness, and those who commit adultery with her into great tribulation, unless they repent of her deeds. And I will kill her children with pestilence, and all the churches will know that I am He who searches the minds and hearts; and I will give to each one of you according to your deeds. But I say to you, the rest who are in Thyatira, who do not hold this teaching, who have not known the deep things of Satan, as they call them—I place no other burden on you. Nevertheless what you have, hold fast until I come. He who overcomes, and he who keeps My deeds until the end, to him I will give authority over the nations; and he shall rule them with a rod of iron, as the vessels of the potter are broken to pieces, as I also have received authority from My Father; and I will give him the morning star. He who has an ear, let him hear what the Spirit says to the churches.'"

Revelation 2:18-29

Repent and Wake Up! Raise Your Awareness and Live Like Jesus will Return Any Day

Once an economic powerhouse, the town of *Sardis* (and the church therein) was deteriorating, but still trying to live off of their former reputation of being strong and alive. There was no remarkable sin or immorality as specified in some of the other churches, but the challenge for them was that they were like the "walking dead." They were unaware, lackluster, and in denial about their true condition. The members of the church gathered together more-so out of habit than to gain fuel to overcome the world. Sardis was a place of gold and wealth, of leisure and lavish living, and a place where intellectual pursuit was highly regarded. Situated high on a hill, they thought they were untouchable. Overconfident, they became too comfortable with existing, while conquering nothing. Jesus told them to wake up and live on this Earth like overcomers. It remains unclear what the dominating spheres in this region and time period were because so much of this city has yet to be excavated. Archaeologists are still working to discover the details of their social culture.

"To the angel of the church in Sardis write: He who has the seven Spirits of God and the seven stars, says this: 'I know your deeds, that you have a name that you are alive, but you are dead. Wake up, and strengthen the things that remain, which were about to die; for I have not found your deeds completed in the sight of My God. So, remember what you have received and heard, and keep it, and repent. Therefore if you do not wake up, I will come like a thief, and you will not know at what hour I will come to you. But you have a few people in Sardis who have not soiled their garments; and they will walk with Me in white, for they are worthy. He who overcomes will thus be clothed in white garments, and I will not erase his name from the book of life, and I will confess his name

before My Father and before His angels. He who has an ear, let him hear what the Spirit says to the churches.'"
Revelation 3:1-6

Repent and Remember the Work I Told You to Do

Laodicea, another economic powerhouse, was quite wealthy and influential due to their production of fine black wool and their manufacturing of pharmaceuticals. The Christian community there blended in so well with non-Christians socially, in business and in play, that they made 'church' just another social club of the day. The church of Laodicea was the 'mega' church in this region, but unfortunately their pride and sense of faultlessness left them too spiritually deaf to comprehend Christ's call to repentance. In their eyes, there was no need for it.

The dominating spheres in this region were business and arts and entertainment.

*"To the angel of the church in Laodicea
write: The Amen, the faithful and true Witness, the
Beginning of the creation of God, says this: 'I know
your deeds, that you are neither cold nor hot; I
wish that you were cold or hot. So because you are
lukewarm, and neither hot nor cold, I will spit you
out of My mouth. Because you say, "I am rich, and
have become wealthy, and have need of nothing,"
and you do not know that you are wretched and
miserable and poor and blind and naked, I advise
you to buy from Me gold refined by fire so that you
may become rich, and white garments so that you
may clothe yourself, and that the shame of your
nakedness will not be revealed; and eye salve to
anoint your eyes so that you may see. Those whom
I love, I reprove and discipline; therefore be zeal-
ous and repent. Behold, I stand at the door and
knock; if anyone hears My voice and opens the
door, I will come into him and will dine with him,
and he with Me. He who overcomes, I will grant to
him to sit down with Me on My throne, as I also
overcame and sat down with My Father on His*

throne. He who has an ear, let him hear what the Spirit says to the churches.'"
Revelation 3:14-22

Jesus was not giving up on any of the churches; He wasn't calling any to close down. He wanted them to know that His power was still present to keep them established and steadfast in the teachings of Christ amidst the trending culture of their day. It was a call to each and every local body and its members to transform (that is, repent and turn back) to the Church that was built upon the fact that "the Kingdom of Heaven was at hand." The need for repentance isn't always because of gross sin; sometimes, it is needed to shake the body of Christ back into the reality of Kingdom-mindedness.

I so clearly see today's local church embodied in all five of these churches in Asia Minor— especially Sardis and Laodicea. In many cases, we're somewhat blind to the fact that we're missing the mark on Christ's intentions for the church, believing the amount of time we spend in the building and/or with the saints means we're hitting the right mark. You may be hearing the knowledge of truth, but are you being transformed by it? Unfortunately, it does not matter how many church services, conferences, workshops, classes, seminars, or mentoring events you attend, until you begin to do things differently, you have not actually received the 'knowledge' you heard. Knowledge must manifest in your choices and behaviors. That's why Jesus said, "He who has an ear, let him hear what the Spirit says to the churches." The look of true repentance is transformation.

Chapter 11

The Conclusion

I opened this book by telling you about Roger Boisjoly, the disciplined craftsman and humble lover of God who *grew* to understand that his life's purpose was to promote ethical awareness in the minds of up-and-coming engineers. The brokenness Boisjoly experienced after being a loud voice crying out against the secret sins of NASA became his turning point - his moment of transformation. George Barna, an expert researcher in the area of church health and spiritual development and founder of the Barna Group, says this:

"Until you experience brokenness you may never transform."

Brokenness propels you to turn away from your customary traditions, activities and habits, because as it's destroying one thing, it's birthing something else. This forces you to stop and think in new ways. Thinking in news ways, when Holy Spirit led, will yield a renewed mind and repentant heart, which will result in a transformed life.

If you were to stand in a room crowded with church-attending Christians and ask, "Who wants to experience brokenness? Please step forward," you will probably find yourself standing alone. Brokenness means emotional pain, suffering, crushing and disruption. Who wants that?

Job said:

"My spirit is broken (bound, destroyed, offended, in ruins), my days are extinguished, The grave is ready for me..."(Job 17:1)

But, then he said:

"Nevertheless the righteous will hold to his way, And he who has clean hands will grow stronger and stronger." (Job 17:9)

David said:

"I am forgotten as a dead man, out of mind; I am like a broken vessel (perished, outcast, displaced, loss of self-worth)..." (Psalm 31:12)

But then he said:

"But as for me, I trust in You, O Lord, I say, 'You are my God.' My times are in Your hand; De-liver me from the hand of my enemies and from those who persecute me." (Psalm 31:14-15)

It is the Lord who heals brokenness, and there is no substitute for His healing. God knows that before you can lead any strong movement of Kingdom advancement, you must be healed of your broken spirit. Proverbs 15:13 says, "A joyful heart makes a cheerful face, but when the heart is sad, the spirit is broken." Proverbs 17:22 says: "...But a broken spirit dries up the bones; it saps your strength."

Included in God's remedy for your bro-kenness is the setting of your feet to walk a new path. When you allow God to heal you complete-ly, brokenness becomes your catalyst for trans-formation. God is ever waiting for that moment when He can give you a total makeover to trans-form you and set you on a new journey. He is al-ways working His purpose in you for His King-dom's sake. So, don't be disheartened by broken-ness; be renewed and transformed because of it.

*While in the throes of brokenness **you can** perceive that a turning point is eminent.*

In his book *Primal Leadership – Realizing the Power of Emotional Intelligence*, Daniel Gole-man shares a story about a man he calls Jurgen. Jurgen was at a point in his professional career where his inability to influence his team to break out of their "work traditions" so they could expe-rience a new level of success left him feeling like dried up bones. If you're anything like me, a lover of God and one who desires to see the Church complete the job Christ told us to finish, you have to ask yourself how well our current "church traditions" are helping us to individually transform, and furthermore, to collectively succeed at advancing the Kingdom throughout the Earth. We have so much unfinished work to do.

In John 19:30, when Jesus said, "It is finished," He was referring to His part of the work—the work of redemption that no other person on Earth would ever be qualified to do. Nevertheless, He was very concerned about us understanding there was still much more work to do. Jesus knew this work would be such a sacrifice that only true lovers of Christ could do. He practically interrogated Simon Peter in John 21:15-17:

- *"Do you love me? ... Tend (properly feed and care for) My lambs."*
- *"Do you love me? ... Shepherd (guide, guard and bring into protection) My sheep."*
- *"Do you love me? ... Tend (properly feed and care for) My sheep."*

(Scriptures taken from Biblehub.com, Strong's Concordance - Greek)

Biblical scholars note the point I'm going to make in a different way, but I believe this: Jesus' sheep are not limited only to the people who place their membership (or followership) in one of our local assemblies. In the local church, we've made the term "sheep" synonymous with members and followers who attend church services on a regular basis. Jesus, however, said this in John 10:11-16:

*"I am the good shepherd; the good shepherd lays down His life for the sheep. He who is a hired hand, and not a shepherd, who is not the owner of the sheep, sees the wolf coming, and leaves the sheep and flees, and the wolf snatches them and scatters them. He flees because he is a hired hand and is not concerned about the sheep. I am the good shepherd, and I know My own and My own know Me, even as the Father knows Me and I know the Father, and I lay down My life for the sheep. **I have other sheep, which are not of this fold; I must bring them also**, and they will hear My voice, and they will become one flock with one shepherd."*

Tending to sheep who are not yet a part of the fold is a major part of Kingdom advancement. It's every believer's job and we should be tending to these sheep in whatever sphere of influence God has positioned us to be in. How you tend to them and shepherd them happens on a person-by-person basis. You cannot draw anyone by force nor by condemnation. Draw them by the love of the Good Shepherd and with the character of our Lord and King.

In order for Kingdom advancement to infiltrate the nations as it should, disciples of Christ must learn the art and skill of *a wise serpent and a harmless dove*. We cannot attend church only to get revived, refilled, delivered and, in many cases, entertained. While all of that is well and good and is very much needed, when we attend church services, we must also gather up *all* we need to be released; that is, released as sheep among wolves and as disciples to the nations. We must know the scriptures more clearly and be able to articulate and dialog about them with non-believers. We must know the ins-and-outs of the sphere of influence God has placed us in, and know the common struggles and evils in those spheres, otherwise, we won't be prepared to discern the wolves, nor to comfort the broken areas in those sheep. We must take our Kingdom calling much more serious than what's become trendy in the local church.

We've witnessed the five churches in Revelations Jesus called to repent because, as they went along with their social and cultural trends, they moved away from the heart of God and from His purpose for the global church.

In his video entitled, "How Lives Are Transformed Part 3," Geroge Barna said: "We (the church) needs to be broken of society, because in our culture right now, the culture influences us more than the ways of God... The culture influences the church more than the church influences the culture."

I believe we can turn this around. It may not be popular now or ever on this side of Heaven, but it's not too late.

Learning Outcomes

Chapter 1: The Challenger's Voice Cries Out

The learner will be able to:
1. Explain what it means to be a "voice crying out in the wilderness."
2. Discuss the concept of "wisdom in the moment."
3. Explain the connection between achieving a goal and discipline.

Chapter 2: Discipline: The Act of Training Your Soulish Man

The learner will be able to:
1. Define discipline.
2. List and explain the three steps in the process of discipline.
3. Explain how "wisdom in the moment" helps your development of discipline.
4. Explain what it means to "train your soulish man."

5. List the questions a person must continually ask himself or herself when training the soulish man.
6. Discuss the out-of-control actions of Simon Peter and how Jesus helped guide him to a more disciplined response.

Chapter 3: Precisely What Is "Kingdom Advancement?"

The learner will be able to:
1. Define "Kingdom advancement."
2. Differentiate between evangelism and outreach.
3. Explain the degree to which words of correction should be given during outreach, evangelism and discipleship.
4. Discuss an exegetical interpretation of Matthew 28:19-20.
5. Explain the connection between Matthew 28:19-20, a transformed life and Kingdom advancement.

Chapter 4: Transformation Happens When We Teach What Jesus Said Teach

The learner will be able to:

1. Define commandment.
2. State what it is Jesus told us to teach the nations.
3. State a primary hindrance to Kingdom advancement.
4. Recognize 35 things Jesus commanded His followers to do.
5. Explain the impact these 35 things should have on our daily lives.

Chapter 5: Kingdom Advancement – A Form of Community Development?

The learner will be able to:

1. Restate what the late Dr. Myles Munroe said about influencing society.
2. Discuss how or why the local church may be viewed as more of a charity than a developer of the community.

3. Discuss how being salt and light is similar to being a leading agent in community development.
4. Discuss which of the 35 commandments can be relative to community development.
5. Explain how Hebrews 10:19-24 and 44-47 reads and implores believers to work.
6. Explain what is meant by the concept of Jesus teaching leaders to be leaders.

Chapter 6: Personal-Development: Becoming Your God-Ordained Self for the Kingdom's Sake

The learner will be able to:
1. Explain the difference between your ideal-self (God-ordained) and your real-self.
2. Explain how personal development relates to becoming your God-ordained self.
3. Discuss what to expect during personal development activities.

4. Discuss which emotions should be resisted during personal development activities.
5. Explain artificial-self worth.
6. Discuss which of the 35 commandments can be relative to personal development.
7. Explain how 1 John 1:8, Ecclesiastes 7:20, and Mathew 5:48 speaks to the idea of personal development and self-worth.
8. List the effects perfectionism can have on one's personal development.
9. Explain how the spirit of pride and self-deception affects personal development.
10. Discuss the analogy of self-deception and "dark corners" as found in Luke 11:34-36 (NLT).

Chapter 7: To Church Leaders – Our Job is To Develop People

The learner will be able to:
1. Explain Pew Research's 2015 findings about church membership and attendance.

2. Explain what should be church leadership's role in developing people.

3. Explain how Matthew 16:18, Matthew 24:4-14, 24 and John 10:7-10 should affect how church leaders should teach the body of Christ.

4. Discuss how Jesus' parable about the Samaritan in Luke 10 informs Christ's followers to respond to problems that we see in our community.

5. Explain Jesus' teaching style, when He taught the 12 disciples, included a teaching style called didactic discourse.

6. Define what is meant by didactic discourse.

7. List the possible reasons why many of today's churches do not use didactic discourse as a teaching style.

8. Discuss the effect fear and insecurity may have on the way ministry leaders teach and develop members of their local church.

9. Explain why Jesus prayed the way He did in John chapter 17.

10. List the four responsibilities of a ministry leader according to 1 Peter 5:1-4.

Chapter 8: Get The 'Christ Perspective' on Leadership

The learner will be able to:

1. Explain what is meant by the statement; "We were all born with a call to leadership."
2. Explain the leadership role God gave to Adam and Eve according to Genesis 2:4-15.
3. Discuss the four things Jesus encountered when it was time for His real earthly work to begin, according to Matthew 4:8-11.
4. Explain what the author means by the phrase "your work," and describe the connection between it and Kingdom advancement.
5. Explain true discipleship, which is the Hebraic perspective of a disciple.
6. Explain why Apostle Paul gained such a notable role in the growth of Christianity.

7. Describe Jesus' pattern for producing leaders.

Chapter 9: Transform

The learner will be able to:
1. List catalysts for transformation.
2. List five things that inhibit a believer from living a transformed life.
3. Differentiate the meaning of repent as was typically used in Old Testament Hebrew versus New Testament Greek.
4. Explain what is the proof a person has accepted the will of God for his or her life.
5. Describe what is needed to attain a transformed life.
6. Describe the two steps involved in the daily renewing of the mind.
7. Explain why the Lord wants to put His law on the believer's heart and mind.
8. Explain the effect that habits have on transformation by a renewed mind.
9. Discuss the correlation between bad habits and strongholds.

10. Explain the effect that prayer, meditation, and knowledge of the word has on the breaking of strongholds.
11. Identify 10 new scripture-based good habits to form when renewing the mind.
12. Explain the correlation between transformation, personal leadership, vision, and empowerment.
13. Explain who and what is our power source, based on the scriptures.
14. State the two visions every person must have before they can successfully lead.

Chapter 10: Transformation, Repentance, and the Five Churches Jesus Rebuked

The learner will be able to:
1. List the names of the five local community churches in Asia Minor who Jesus called to repent, according to the book of Revelations.
2. Describe the societal norms of the cities where each of the five churches were located.

3. Explain how the local church responded to the societal norms.
4. State the reason(s) each church was called to repent.
5. State the correlation between each society and the most likely dominating sphere of influence in each city.
6. State the name and reason of the one church who was promised a severe punishment if they failed to repent.

Chapter 11– The Conclusion

The learner will be able to:

1. Explain church faith expert George Barna's viewpoint on transformation.
2. Describe how Job and David renewed their minds during times of brokenness.
3. Explain why one must overcome and use brokenness for the Kingdom's sake.
4. Discuss the how "tending sheep" in John 10:11-16 may relate to Kingdom advancement.

Sources

Chapter 1

1. Howard Berkes, "Remembering Roger Boisjoly: He Tried To Stop Shuttle Challenger Launch," *NPR*, 2012, February 6, http://www.npr.org/sections/thetwo-way/2012/02/06/146490064/remembering-roger-boisjoly-he-tried-to-stop-shuttle-challenger-launch

2. Ibid.

3. Cory Frankly, "Remembering the Passed - In memoriam Roger Boisjoly," 2012, March 23, https://www.youtube.com/watch?v=nR2GkhypoBI

4. Ibid.

5. Joseph Trento, "Roger Boisjoly – The Conscience of Engineering," *DC Bureau*, 2012, February 13. http://www.dcbureau.org/201202137027/trentos-take/roger-boisjoly-the-conscience-of-engineering.html

6. Douglas Martin, "Roger Boisjoly, 73, Dies; Warned of Shuttle Danger", *New York*

Times, 2012, February 2,
http://www.nytimes.com/2012/02/04/u
s/roger-boisjoly-73-dies-warned-of-
shuttle-danger.html?_r=0

7. *Online Ethics Center for Engineering*
"Roger Boisjoly Curriculum Vitae," 2016,
August 29,
www.onlineethics.org/Topics/ProfPractic
e/Exemplars/BehavingWell/RB-
intro/33759/CurriculumVitae.aspx

Chapter 3

1. *Urban Dictionary*, "Sunday Funday"
http://www.urbandictionary.com/define.
php?term=sunday%20funday

2. Tim Challies, "Evangelism & Outreach."
Challies, 2004, November 9,
http://www.challies.com/articles/evange
lism-outreach

3. Ibid.

4. Myles Munroe, "The Leading Edge
Leadership Show #4, 2013 October 3,
https://youtu.be/e_tvKEk8-OE

Chapter 5

1. Myles Munroe, "Three foundational principles for discovering personal leadership," Dr Myles Munroe, 2014, April 26, https://youtu.be/lpl2DlbiKw0

2. Flo Frank and Anne Smith, "What is Community Development? By The Community Development Handbook: A Tool to Build Community Capacity", *PeerNetBC.* http://www.peernetbc.com/what-is-community-development#sthash.TbDuag6i.5zpTHzmM.dpuf

Chapter 6

1. Daniel Goleman, *Primal Leadership – Realizing the Power of Emotional Intelligence*, Boston, MA: Harvard Business School Publishing, 2002, page 111

2. Ibid.

Chapter 7

1. Pew Research Group. "America's Changing Religious Landscape," 2015, May 12, http://www.pewforum.org/2015/05/12/americas-changing-religious-landscape/

2. Sierra Wendt, "Be The Change You Want to See in Your Church," *Ferver*, 2013, September 27, http://fervr.net/bible/be-the-change-you-want-to-see-in-your-church

3. Bruce Booker, "Discipleship: Walking like the Master," *Beth Yeshua Messianic Congregation*, 2008, http://www.bethyeshua-idaho.com/brbooker/discipleship.html

Chapter 8

1. Myles Munroe, "The Leadership Philosophy Of Jesus," 2012, December 16, https://youtu.be/aa94LjxmY_k

2. Bruce Booker, "Discipleship: Walking like the Master," *Beth Yeshua Messianic Congregation*, 2008,

http://www.bethyeshua-
idaho.com/brbooker/discipleship.html

Chapter 9

1. S, Coates and D Schechter, "Preschoolers'
    traumatic stress post-9/11: Relational
    and developmental perspectives",
    Psychiatric Clinics of North America, 27
    (3): 473–489.

2. Statistic Brain. "9/11 Death Statistics",
    2016, August 1,
    http://www.statisticbrain.com/911-
    death-statistics/

3. By The Fiscal Policy Institute. "The
    Employment Impact of the September 11
    World Trade Center Attacks: Updated
    Estimates based on the Benchmarked
    Employment Data", 2002, March 8,
    http://www.fiscalpolicy.org/Employment
    %20Impact%20of%20September
    %2011_Update.pdf

4. The New World Trade Center,
    https://wtc.com/media/press-kit

5. Art Markman, "# 122: How to Help People Change", *Engaging Leader Podcast,* 2015, October 15,
    http://www.engagingleader.com/122-how-to-help-people-change-podcast/?utm_source=feedburner&utm_medium=feed&utm_campaign=Feed%3A+EngagingLeader+%28Engaging+Leader+Podcast+%28EL%29%29

6. Beth Moore, *Breaking Free*, (Nashville, TN: B&H Publishing Group, 2000), 240-241.

7. Myles Munroe, "The Leading Edge Leadership Show #1", 2013, September 27, https://youtu.be/l4ezu2TquMw

8. David Oyedepo, *Leadership Part 1*. 2011, March 3, https://youtu.be/KYFqBrYWVBA

Chapter 10

1. Bible Study Tools. 15.1, "Why these Seven Churches", http://www.biblestudytools.com/comme

ntaries/revelation/related-topics/why-these-seven-churches.html

2. Bible Study Tools. 15.1.1, "Representative of All Churches of All Ages", http://www.biblestudytools.com/commentaries/revelation/related-topics/representative-of-all-churches-of-all-ages.html

3. Agape Bible Study, "Revelation Chapter 2, Pergamum (3)", http://www.agapebiblestudy.com/Revelation/Chapter%202%20Pergamum.htm

4. Bible.org, "Pergamum - The Compromising Church", https://bible.org/seriespage/4-pergamum-compromising-church

5. BeyondTodayTV, "The Churches of Revelation: Pergamos - The Compromising Church", 2015, July 16, https://youtu.be/B3CFaJ97TOE

6. BeyondTodayTV, "The Churches of Revelation: Sardis - The Dead Church", 2015, August 13, https://youtu.be/WGAUmZeleUw

7. Cristian Violatti, "Ancient History Encyclopedia – Sardis", 2014, March 20, http://www.ancient.eu/sardis/

8. The Archaeological Exploration of Sardis, "About Sardis", 2015, http://www.sardisexpedition.org/en/essays/about-sardis

Chapter 11

1. George Barna,, "How Lives Are Transformed – Maximum Faith Part 3", 2012, April 30, https://youtu.be/MTJtABHuWiI

2. Daniel Goleman, *Primal Leadership – Realizing the Power of Emotional Intelligence*, (Boston, MA: Harvard Business School Publishing, 2002, page 125-126

3. Biblehub.com, Strong's Concordance - Greek 1006. Boskó. http://biblehub.com/greek/1006.htm

4. Biblehub.com, Strong's Concordance – Greek 4165. Poimainó, http://biblehub.com/greek/4165.htm

5. Biblehub.com, Strong's Concordance - Greek 1006. Boskó, http://biblehub.com/greek/1006.htm